©2013 Andrea Maglio-Macullar
No part of this book may be copied,
downloaded, used in any other publication or
otherwise without the written permission
of the author and publisher.

Modern Saints
of the Catholic Faith

Introduction

    I have always been very interested in the Saints of our wonderful Catholic faith, especially, the newest. These holy, beautiful souls are our friends and heavenly intercessors. They have tirelessly, lived their lives for God. These people have given over their lives, and have given up many comforts and pleasures to save others. As St. Jacinta Marto did, the youngest child Saint none martyred. Who was a natural singer and dancer, gave this joy up, after seeing visions of hell. She was totally convinced that she should do penance, pray and make many sacrifices for poor sinners. We can also call on them when we feel we need some help in our daily lives they are there for us to gladly help us. Just ask them, you will not be disappointed.

    I think we all need to read and learn about these faith filled people. God has given them to us, to help us, especially when times are difficult, or they are not going our way. We need to see what others did when their lives were difficult. I pray this book will help young and old alike to see God's Glory through these holy people's lives and also help point us average folks in the right direction, Heavenward.

    They are great models for us today. We need to learn and sit quietly, listening to what our Heavenly Father wants from us. This is truly where we will be the happiest on this earth, doing and trusting in God's Holy will.

Thank you again for purchasing and reading this book. I look forward to meeting you all in heaven someday (I pray) Also, if you have found favor with this book please write a short review from the page on Amazon/Kindle. It will help others know about the saints and help them get to heaven too.

Table of Contents

St. Jacinta Marto
St. Francisco Marto
St Teresa of the Andes
St. Josephine Bakhita
Blessed Elizabeth of the Trinity
St. Pio of Pietrelcina
St. Gemma Galgani
Bl. Pier Giorgio Frassati
St. Therese of Lisieux
St. Maria Faustina Kawalska
St. Gianna Beretta Molla
St. Teresa Benedicta of the Cross
St. Maximilian Kolbe

St. Jacinta Marto 1910-1920
St. Francisco Marto 1908-1919

Saints, Jacinta and Francisco were siblings. They were two of the shepherd children from Fatima, Portugal, to whom the Blessed Mother appeared six times, starting May 13, 1917 until October 1917, on the 13th of each month. They were the sixth and seventh in the Marto family. Being illiterate, they were humble and simple. The took care of the sheep with their cousin, Lucia Santos. (Sister Lucia)

Our Lady showed the children a vision of hell during one of the apparitions. After this sight, Jacinta being a very light hearted child. She had a natural gift to dance and had a voice to sing. Jacinta gave this up. Deciding to pray and do self-mortification. They
were convinced that penance and sacrifice was needed to save poor sinners, like us.

They both died as children of the influenza epidemic of 1918. Francisco was 11years old and Jacinta was 10.

Their feast day is February 20th. They are patrons of illness,

captives, people ridiculed for their faith, sickness and against sickness.

They were beatified May 13, 2000 the feast of Our Lady of Fatima, by Pope John Paul II. Jacinta is the youngest non martyred Saint to be canonized.

St Teresa of the Andes

St. Teresa of the Andes was from Santiago, Chile. She was the first Saint from that region of the world. She was born on July 13, 1900, and Baptized on July 15, 1900, at St. Ann's Church in Santiago. Her name was Juanita. She was the fifth child in her family. They were very wealthy; Her Paternal grandfather came from Spain. They lived on a very large estate. She attended The Theresian Sister's School, also in Santiago. At the age of six, Juanita had a very strong desire to receive her first communion. People thought she was too young. She was very close to and had great love for her family.

In 1907 the little saint became a day student at The Sacred Heart School. Her brother teaches her to pray the Rosary that she prayed every day of her life except one, when she forgot.

It was 1910 when Juanita got to receive her first Communion. The whole year before this she made many sacrifices to prepare herself. Her communion had a great impression on her life. She tried to receive Jesus almost every day thereafter.

In 1914, Juanita had a very difficult year she had her appendix removed. At the time this was a very delicate, dangerous surgery. She also read The Story of a Soul, the great Spiritual classic of St. Therese of Lisieux, this is before St. Therese is beatified. This is also the time she feels Christ calling her to be totally His.

Juanita becomes a boarding student in 1915 at the Sacred Heart School with her sister Rebecca. She starts to keep a diary. On December 8th of that year she takes a temporary vow of chastity. She promised, to have no other spouse than Jesus. She wanted to serve Him for her whole life and whom she loved with all her heart.

In 1917 her family has financial problems and they have to sell their estate. Jaunita receives a medal as a Child of Mary. She reads a book about Elizabeth of the Trinity another Carmelite nun. She also makes a general confession and is found not to have any
mortal sins. At this time she writes to the Carmel at Los Andes and would like to join the Sisters.

Jaunita receives many awards at school in 1918. She spends her summer on the Pacific shore teaching Catechism and choir. In

September she returns to her family and gets a positive answer from the Carmel. She receives the name Teresa of Jesus. She reads the book by St. Teresa of Avilla. Sr. Teresa suffers from separation from her family but her soul is filled with great joy & peace to live the life at Carmel.

1919 was a year Sr. Teresa knows her life will soon end. She suffers much, having Typhus.

She dies at the Carmel in 1920, not even 20 years old.

John Paul 2 calls her venerable, March 22, 1986 Beatified, Teresa de Los Andes.

1993 Canonized, March 21, St. Peters Rome, by Pope John Paul 2. Her feast day is July 13.

St. Josephine Bakhita

St. Josephine Bakhita was born in Olgossa, Darfur, Sudan, Africa in 1869.To a very wealthy Sudanese family. She was kidnapped at a young age and sold into child slavery. Many times bought, sold and beaten. So much that she forgot her name her parents gave her. "Bakhita" her name means "fortunate". Her kidnappers gave this to her. She experienced many times the suffering and embarrassment of slavery, moral and physical.

Bakhita was eventually bought by an Italian Consul, Callisto Legnani. He wanted to free her, taking her to Italy. This was the first time in her life that no one lashed her. They treated her with love and kindness.   She stayed with friends of the Consuls, family, The
Michieli family. Mrs. Michieli wanted Bakhita to be baby sitter or nanny for their daughter, Mimmina. She became one of the family.

The two became enrolled in school of the Daughters of Charity. The "Canossian Sisters in Venice. Here she learned about the Catholic faith. Mrs. Michieli wanted to go back to Sudan. They sold their house and while the Michieli's went back to Sudan, Bakhita and Mimmina remained with the Canossian Sisters. When they returned from Sudan, Bakhita would not leave the sisters convent.

In 1890 Bakhita was baptized as a Catholic, and took the name Josephine, for her new life in Christ. Every day she became more in love with God in whom she knew was leading her by the hand. She became an adult in Italy where she could be free as Italian law would let her.

Josephine eventually felt called to Religious life. She entered the Institute of St Magdalene of Canossa. On December

8, 1896, she was consecrated forever to God.
Josephine continued to live there humbly, for the next 50 years. At the community of the Sisters of Charity in Schio, A part of Vicenza, Venice. She cooked and served, did embroidery, answered the door. Bakhita was a very loving, kind woman. The people of the city grew to love her. She gave some talks around Italy and was told to write her memoirs. These talks made her famous in Italy. She had a wonderful, kindness about her that drew others to Jesus. The people of the town got great comfort from her kind voice and manner. They called her a saint.

    The last years of her life were filled with physical pain and suffering. Her delirium brought her back to days of slavery. Bakita would scream out to loosen the heavy chains.
Josephine died on February 8th 1947, at the convent where she lived. Many people came to pay their respects to her.

    The cause for her canonization began soon after her death. The process started in 1959. Then on December 9, 1978 Pope John Paul II declared her Venerable. May 7, 1992 was declared, blessed. And on October 1, 2000 She became a Saint, by Pope John Paul II.
Her feast day is February 8th. She is the patroness of Slavery and Oppression. She is a modern day African Saint. The patron Saint of Sudan.

Blessed Elizabeth of the Trinity

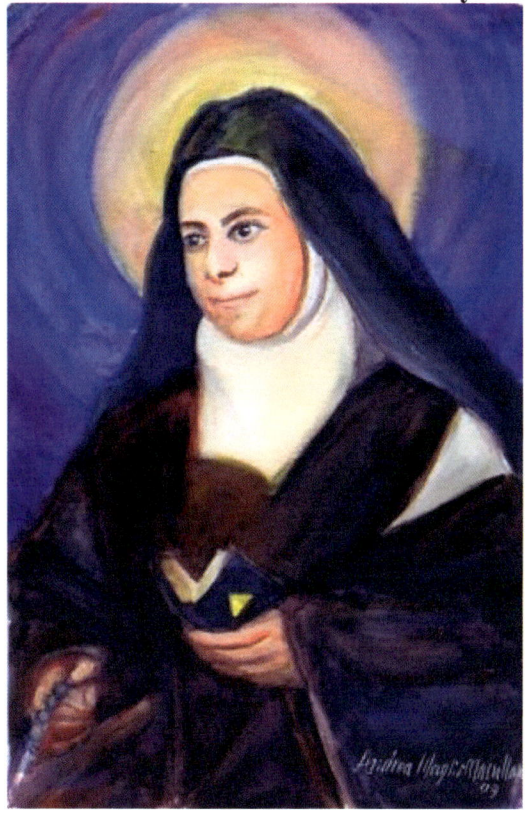

This young Blessed is on Her way to being Saint Elizabeth of the Trinity. Her name was Elizabeth Catez. Elizabeth's nickname was "Sabeth". She was born on a Sunday, on July 18, 1880, at a military camp in Bourges, France. When she was seven, her father died. He was Captain Joseph Catez. Elizabeth was left with her mother, Marie Catez and her younger sister, Marguerite.   She was a very stubborn child and a gifted pianist. After her first Communion in 1891, she became more introspective, more understanding of God.

 Sabeth was a very lively and popular girl, winning many awards for her musical talents.

 In the year 1894, she heard an interior call to be a Carmelite. She made a private vow of perpetual virginity. At the age of 21, Elizabeth's mother agrees to let her enter Carmel and has her first visit. She teaches catechism to children, and visits the sick, Elizabeth also had a great prayer life.

 She entered the Carmel in Dijon, France, about 200 miles from where she lived. Her stay there had some good and not so good times. These experiences gave Elizabeth a deeper understanding of God's love.

 In 1903 she took her final vows, after completing her novitiate. Much of her life was spent writing many letters and guides for retreats. She was also a spiritual director to many people. For the next few years she had much spiritual and physical suffering.

In 1905 she was diagnosed with Addison's disease. This affects the endocrine system. At first she was missed diagnosed. Doctors were not sure of her illness, this caused her much pain.

 Elizabeth died a year later in 1906. She was only 26 years old and had a great understanding of the Holy Trinity. Her beatification was on November 25, 1984, the feast
of Christ the King, by Pope John Paul II.

 She is patron of sick people, illness and loss of parents.

St. Pio of Pietrelcina

St. Padre Pio was born on May 25, 1887. The name he was give was Francesco Forgione.
His parents were Giuseppa and Grazio Forgione. They lived in a small farming town, east of Naples in Southern Italy, near Benevento, called Pietrelcina. He had an older brother, Michele and three younger sisters, Felicita, Pellegrina and Grazia. His family did not have much money, but they were wealthy in their Catholic faith.

Padre Pio said by the age of five he decided to give his life to God. He also started to do penances, as sleeping on the floor and using a rock for a pillow. He worked on the land for his family. Taking care of a small flock of sheep they owned. He started school a little later than most children because of this.

The town where Padre Pio came from was very religious, most people there were illiterate, but they memorized bible stories and the scriptures that others would tell them.
He also said that he would speak with Jesus, our Blessed Mother and his Guardian Angel.
He experienced heavenly visions and ecstasies and thought all others did also.

In 1897 Francesco finished 3 years of public school and became interested in being a Capuchin friar. He visited a friary 13 miles north in Morcone to see if he was eligible.
Francesco was told he could enter but he needed more education. His family had a private tutor give him lessons so he could get the qualifications needed. At this time Francesco received his Confirmation. It was September 27, 1899 at the age of 15
On January 6, 1903, He entered the novitiate of the Capuchin Fathers of Marcone.

This is when he got the habit and the name Brother Pio. He also took vows of poverty, chastity and obedience. His name was to honor Pope St. Pius V, patron Saint of Pietrelcina.

In 1910 Brother Pio was ordained a Priest in the Cathedral of Benevento. After this time his health was not good he went back to his home town. He was living again with his family he taught school and said Mass. Eventually; he was called back to San Giovanni
Rotondo, a community of seven other friars. He stayed here the rest of his life. Here he was a spiritual director to many and he had a growing reputation for working miracles,
Reading people's hearts, hearing confessions for many hour at a time. He tried to teach other to see God in all things and to do God's will always.

In 1911 Padre Pio received the Stigmata. These are the five wounds Christ suffered during His crucifixion. He experienced this painfully for the 50 years of his life.
He also had many spiritual gifts, bilocation, and levitation; prophesy, miracles, conversions,
and a wonderful fragrance from his wounds.

He also built a hospital in 1940, for the suffering. It was built on the mountain next to the monastery in San Giovanni Rotondo In the 1960 Padre Pio health declines, he became weaker, although he was always a man of great faith and God filled his life. Padre Pio was always concerned about others. He had an amazing prayer life, almost always in conversation with God. He said that "Prayer is the key that opens God's heart" at all times he had great hope and trust in God and wanted others to love and trust also. The Saint accepted everything that happened as God's

permitting will and was obedient.
     In 1968 the stigmata he bore started to disappear. During his last Mass he could hardly stand and sometimes they went on for hours. Padre Pio Dies on September 23. He was 81.   Tens of thousands of people attend his funeral. Evan after his death miracles were attributed to him. In 1999 Padre Pio was beatified by Pope John Paul II on May 2.
He was canonized on June 16 2002, also by Pope John Paul II. His feast day is September 23. Saint Pio is the patron of Civil Defense workers.

St. Gemma Galgani

Gemma was born on March 12, 1878. In Camigliano, Italy. She was the fifth child in a family of eight children. She was oldest of the girls. Her father was a Pharmacist and was very good at it. Gemma's mother was a very religious woman, she taught Gemma at a very young age to love prayer and the Catholic faith. Even at five years old, she was devoted to Our Blessed Mother and wanted to learn about Jesus.

The Galganni family lived in a small village outside of Lucca, in Tuscany in central Italy. When Gemma was eight, her mother died of tuberculosis. She was a very saintly example to her. After her mother's death, Gemma was sent to a school where the Sisters of St. Zita taught. The sisters helped her along in her spiritual life. They taught her to meditate and have devotion to the Passion of Jesus. She prays fifteen decades of the Rosary daily on her knees and does penance.

Being the eldest daughter in her family much of the work at home fell on her shoulders, cooking and cleaning and caring for the other children in her family. She also helped teach other children in the town, religious education, and would make alter cloths. Gemma had a joyous loving spirit. She would also visit the sick and poor and give them their needs and an inspiring word about God.

Gemma received her confirmation at seven years old, and Jesus spoke to her in an inner locution. Jesus asked her if he could take her mother to heaven, she said yes and wanted to go also. Jesus said not yet. When Gemma was 9 she received her first communion.

Gemma's brother Gino with whom she was very close was studying to be a priest. During this time he also became ill of tuberculosis and died in 1894. Then a few years later in 1897, her father also became ill of cancer and died. The rest of family was left with no money. Gemma started working for the Giannini family. She cleaned their home and helped with the chores and at 21, she was adopted by them. This family was very well off. Gemma at about this time developed a curvature of the spine that was very painful; she had to wear a back brace that kept her spine in line. Jesus gave her a great grace, His holy wounds, The Stigmata. Her hands and feet would bleed on certain days of the week. She would have conversations with her Guardian angel, he would appear to her and they would pray together and meditate on Jesus' Passion.

Gemma had a great devotion to the venerable Gabriel of The Sorrowful Mother. After a novena to the Sacred Heart of Jesus, Gemma was cured of her back pain. It was through St. Gabriel intervention, that Jesus healed her.

In 1902 she became ill again and she had a spiritual dryness. She had no consolation in her prayer. She suffered so much physically and spiritually with great heroic patience. Gemma never complained. Her illness took its toll on her body, but she was still beautiful to the end of her life.

Gemma died on April 11, 1903. She was 25 years old. She was beatified by Pope Pius XI and Canonized in 1940 on May2. Only 37 years after her death.

Bl. Pier Giorgio Frassati

Man of the Eight Beatitudes

Pier Giorgio Frassati was born on April 6, 1901 in Turin, Italy. His family was very comfortable money wise, though his father was very frugal and a very influential Italian Politician. He was senator, and then an ambassador to Germany. He was also the founder of the newspaper "La Stampa". His mother was an artist, the painter Adelaide Amatis.
Pier Giorgio had a younger sister too, Luciana.

Pier Giorgio developed a deep spiritual life at a young age. He got permission to receive Jesus in the Blessed Sacrament every day. This was very unusual for his time.

He would not hesitate to help others at any time. Pier Giorgio was also a great athlete, his friends and he would get together and go on mountain climbing trips, but first they would go to Mass. He was a very average young man and lived a very average life. He showed us that you can be holy in all aspects of your life. He was very sensitive to the needs of others. He lead youth groups and other Catholic groups, at seventeen he joined the St. Vincent de Paul Society. Pier Giorgio was an average student, he liked to play practical jokes on his friends. He became very involved with political groups. He was against Fascism, and he always worked for the Catholic Churches social teaching.

When Pier Giorgio was 21 he became a third order Dominican or a secular Dominican. He took the name Girolamo or Jerome. Money that his parents would give him he would use for the poor. He would ride the train in third class, instead of first and give the extra money to those who had no money to ride the train.

He always had great concern for the needy and the sick. Pier Giorgio would visit them tending to their needs. One cold day he was with his father in Germany, he saw a man cold and shivering and gave away his coat to him. His father was very angry about this.

This was the type of person Pier Giorgio was.

In College he studied to be an Engineer. He wanted to help the people who worked in the mine as miners, bringing them a safer way to work.

One day, as he was visiting the sick, he contracted polio, a disease that paralyzes the body. It took hold of him very quickly and within a week he was paralyzed. Pier Giorgio died on July 4 1925. He was only 24 years old.

Pope John Paul II called him the man of the 8 beatitudes, when he was beatified on May 20, 1990. His body was exhumed and found incorrupt. Now he is buried in the Turin Cathedral, the same place as they keep the Holy Shroud.

Pier Giorgio is a great witness to our faith. He shows us that holiness is attainable for all people.

St. Therese of Lisieux
The Little Flower

Patroness of the missions Doctor of The Church and "The Little Way"

    St. Therese of Lisieux was born January 2, 1873 in Alencon France. She was baptized Marie-Françoise-Thérèse Martin. She was the youngest of the children of Louis and Zelie Martin. Who are also on their way to become Saints.
Therese lost her mother to breast cancer at four years old. She became

withdrawn, shy and serious. She said to her oldest sister Pauline that she would be her Mama now.   Therese found it very difficult to be at school.

She would go with her sisters to study at the Benedictine Abby School of Notre Dame. Therese said these were the saddest years in her life. When she was 10 years old her sister Pauline decided she would become a Carmelite nun. At this time Therese became very ill for several weeks.

This was very upsetting for her family. Therese could not eat or sleep very

well and was fearful. When Therese 'illness seemed to be at the worst ever, all her sisters prayed by her bedside to Our Blessed Mother. They had a statue of Our Lady of the Smile. Therese said that Our Lady Smiled at her and Therese was cured.

 When Therese was 11 she said she felt her first "call" to the Religious life. She wanted to be united to Jesus as a Carmelite. Therese did have to wait until she was 15 which is very young to enter Religious Life. It was 1888 when Therese entered the Carmel of Lisieux. Her life did not all of a sudden become perfect, but the convent was perfect for her life. She lost all consolation at prayer and sometimes would fall asleep during it. Her father was very ill at this time too and entered a mental hospital. This greatly distressed all the Martin sisters. Celine would take care of their father. Therese's father passed on to heaven on July 29, 1894, a very sad day for all the Martin family.

 Celine entered the Carmel a few months after their father's death. She brought her camera with her .At the time photography was just starting to become popular and affordable to everyone. Celine took many pictures of Therese. This is why there are so many photos of the little Saint.

 Therese was the novice mistress teaching all the new women that came to live and become Nun's. She was also a Sacristan. She lived her little way of love every day. She had faith and trust in God that He would take care of her.

 Therese became ill with Tuberculosis in 1896. Pauline, her older sister was the prioress, she told Therese to write down her memories in a journal. This is where Therese wrote all her life story and her thoughts of her faith and beliefs. Therese' "Little Way" she described here. It was to do things no matter how small with great love. She also wrote that her vocation was "love". During this time as Therese became more and more sick and week, she would never let anyone know how much she was suffering. She remained cheerful and happy, some of the nun's thought she was faking her sickness because she didn't seem ill to the others.

Therese prophetically knew at this time that she was getting close to her death and knew that she would come down, she said .She would spend her heaven doing good things for the people on earth..

Therese was now spending the last days of her life in the infirmary in the Carmel of Lisieux. On September 30, 1897, at the age of 24, Therese passed from this world to heaven. Her "Little Way" and her books of writing were published for the others nuns of the Carmels in France. They were very popular. Then they were published for the public and were read all over the world. Therese' writings "The Story of a Soul" remains until today one of the most read and loved Spiritual books. St Therese is one of the most popular and loved Saints of all time. Please, St. Therese, our beautiful sister in Christ. Pray to Jesus for us.

St. Maria Faustina Kawalska

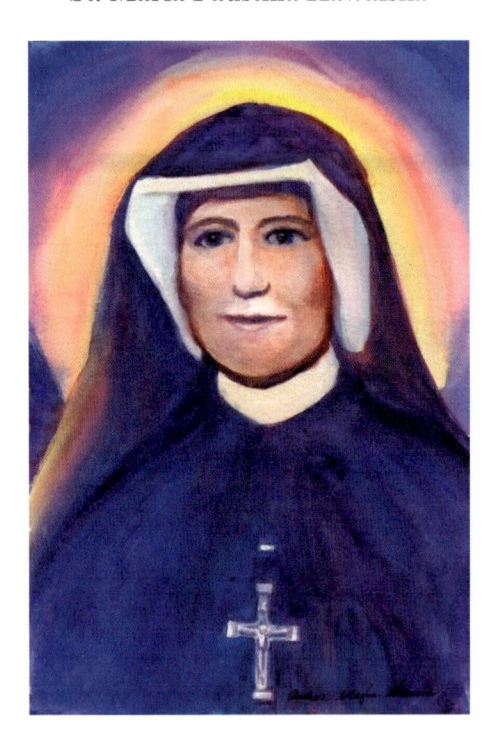

St. Faustina was born on August 5, 1905. She was named Helenka Kowalska, near the town of Lodz, Poland. She came from a large family, the 3rd of 1o children. They were a poor peasant family. Helenka first heard the call to Religious life when she was just 7 years old. She wanted to enter the convent when she finished her education but her parents would not let her. At 16 years old she had to go to work as a house cleaner to help support her family and herself. Helenka was at a dance when she was 19 and had a vision of the suffering Jesus. She left right away and went to the Cathedral, where Jesus told her to enter the convent in Warsaw. She left for Warsaw not telling her family. She visited many convents but no one wanted her. After a few weeks of searching, she met the Mother Superior of the Sisters of Our Lady of Mercy. The Mother Superior decided to accept her on one condition that she would have to pay for her habit. Helenka worked for a year as a maid to raise the funds. On April 30, 1926 at age 20, her name became Sister Maria Faustina of The Blessed Sacrament. In April 1929 she took her first vows.

    Sister Fautina met Fr. Sopocko, He was the Confessor for all the Nuns in the convent. She confided in him that she was receiving messages from Jesus. Fr. Sopocko told Sr. Faustina to keep a diary and write all the messages down. She also told her confessor that Jesus wanted her to have a painting done of the Divine Mercy image. They did have a painter paint the image and Faustina complained to Jesus that no one could paint you as beautiful as you really are, and Jesus said" 'not in the beauty of the color, nor of the brush is the greatness of this image, but in my grace.'" ...

    Sr. Faustina's life was one of great sacrifice and suffering. She lived to do the will of God. She continued to speak and have visions of Jesus all her life. She delivered the message of Divine Mercy that Jesus wants the world to know.

    Jesus told St. Faustina to tell us that we must Trust in Jesus, and His Mercy.
Believe that Jesus *is All Mercy.* Jesus said that anyone that venerates the Divine Mercy image will not perish.

    Sister Faustina became very ill during the last 2 years of her life with Tuberculosis. She died on October 5, 1938. Pope John Paul II beatified Sr. Faustina on April 18 1993 and he canonized her on April 30, 2000.

St. Gianna Beretta Molla

St. Gianna is a profile Saint. She was also a Mother, a Wife and a Doctor. This very holy woman Saint of modern times lived a very virtuous life every day.

She was born in Magenta, Italy on October 4, 1922. A few days later on October 11th, Gianna was baptized in the Basilica of St. Martino also in Magenta. She was the 10th of thirteen children. Her parents were 3rd order Franciscans or today they are called, Secular Franciscans. The Beretta family lived with great simplicity and joy. They would go to Mass very early every morning. Gianna's parents wanted their children to be well educated so they could serve others and be good examples of Christian life.

Gianna received her first Holy Communion at 5 years old; this was a truly wonderful experience for her. She then loses her oldest sister Amelia at 14 years old. Her sister died of being sick for a long time. This brought much suffering into Gianna's life. She loved and missed her sister Amelia greatly. In 1938 Gianna's father moved their family to Genoa, so they could be near the university. Gianna and her sister, Virginia, attended a secondary school run by the Dorothean Sisters. At this time she also made an Ignatian retreat.
Gianna learned mental prayer and a horror for sin. She never wanted to hurt our Blessed Jesus with sin, she would rather die. She wanted to offer Jesus everything.

In 1942, Gianna lost both her parents, first her mother and then her father 4 months later. After her graduation from high school, Gianna wanted to become a medical missionary in Brazil where her brother was a Priest. This never happened. Gianna stated Medical school in Milan and in 1949 she got her diploma. She then opens an office near Magenta, specializing in Pediatrics.

In December1954 She met Pietro Molla. They became friends and eventually married in September 1955. They started a family, having 3 children. They then lost 2 babies in miscarriage. Gianna then is pregnant again in 1962. She developed complications. Gianna makes it known to save the life of her child first. Her last child was born by caesarian section and was healthy. Gianna was not doing so well. She developed and infection from the operation and passed on to heaven 7 days after her baby was born. If this was in the present day more than likely Gianna would not have died, because medicine is more advanced now.

Gianna was beatified by Pope John Paul II on April 24, 1994

and canonized in on May16, 2004. Her husband and some of her children were present at the ceremony. She is the patron saint of Mothers, Physicians and preborn children.

St. Teresa Benedicta of the Cross

Edith Stein

Edith Stein was born in 1891. She came from a very devote Jewish family. She was the youngest of 11 children. Her father died when she was only 2 years old. Edith had a great passion for learning and showed a great aptitude for it. Her mother, even though she was widowed, wanted her children to still have an excellent education. Edith went to study at the University of Bresslau. At this time in her life she purposely decided not to pray any more, becoming an atheist. She went on to study at the University of Gottingen, and in 1916 received a doctorate in philosophy. Her dissertation was under the philosopher Edmund Husserl. He led many students to the Catholic faith. Edith eventually became a teacher at the University of Freiburg. Here, she was an assistant to Husserl. Edith was a suffragette at this time. She was all for women and their rights, and at this time she started to read many books on the Catholic faith. One of her favorites was St. Theresa of Avilla. This caused her conversion to the Catholic faith. She was baptized in 1922. Edith then became a teacher at the Catholic school run by the Dominican Nuns. She taught there for several years and while there, she translated St. Thomas Aquinas' De Vertate into German.

She was becoming more and more familiar with Catholic philosophy.

    Edith entered the Discalced (means without shoes) Carmelite Monastery in Cologne, called Our Lady of Peace, in 1933. Her name became Teresa Benedicta of the Cross. During this time she wrote a metaphysical book (Metaphysics is a science that helps people understand the world)called *Finite and Eternal Being*. Teresa tried to combine the philosophies of St. Thomas Aquinas and Edmond Husserl.

    Soon after this time it was not safe for Teresa to be at this Monastery, so she was transferred to the Monastery in Echt, in the Netherlands. This was because the Nazis were a threat. Teresa's sister was also with her and wanted to become a Catholic. Eventually too, the sisters were not safe in the Netherlands either. The Nazis arrested them at the Monastery. They were sent to Auschwitz, where they gassed with many other people that day. St. Teresa Benedicta died a true Martyr of the faith.

    St. Teresa's feast day is August 9th. She was Beatified on May 1,

1987 and Canonized October 11, 1998, both by Pope John Paul II.

St. Maximilian Kolbe
The Apostle of Consecration to Mary

St. Maximilian Kolbe was born Raymond Kolbe on January 8, 1894. He lived in the town of Zdunska Wola in Poland. He was the second of 5 brothers. His parents were very simple, humble people.
They would weave baskets and grow vegetables. His father was eventually captured and hanged by the Russians because he joined the Prime Minister of Poland and fought for the Independence for a Partitioned Poland.

When Raymond was very young he said he had a vision of The Blessed Mother. Our Lady showed him two crowns, one was white for purity and one was red for Martyrdom. Our Mother asked him which he wanted. Raymond chose both. This vision had a very strong impact on his life. He then knew he was destined for martyrdom. In 1907 Raymond and his elder brother decided to join the Conventual Franciscans. This was a minor Seminary in Lwow.

He excelled in all his subjects. He loved the sciences and designed a space ship a lot like the ones NASA has built. He was a very brilliant man, earning, 2 doctorate degrees in Philosophy and Theology. In 1910 he was received as a novice and got the name Maximilian. Later in 1917, Maximilian was ordained on April 28th.

After he was ordained he returned to Poland. He then taught in the Seminary, and became a publisher and printer of many periodicals and a daily newspaper. Fr. Kolbe got permission to build
A monastery in Warsaw called Niepokalanow. It was the City of the Immaculata. It was one the largest seminaries anywhere. Over 700 Religious men lived there, during the 2nd World war it housed many injured soldiers and Fr. Kolbe housed and hid many Jewish people there also.

In 1930 Fr. Kolbe went to Japan and built another Monastery
in Nagasaki. There, he also published a Japanese newspaper.
In 1941, Fr. Kolbe went back to Poland at this time he was trying to save many Jews from the Nazis. In February that year, the saint was arrested and sent to Pawiak prison. Then in May he was sent to Auschwitz. Here was beaten and terribly humiliated. One day one of the prisoners escaped, that meant that 10 prisoners would die. One of the men was a young, husband and father, and Fr. Kolbe asked to
take his place.

Fr. Kolbe would say Mass every day in the prison. He would hear people's confession and consoling them. He tried to keep the moral of the people high, by singing spiritual songs and with prayer.

One day, a guard thought it was taking to long for Fr. Kolbe to die. They gave him a lethal injection.Fr. Maximilian died on August
14, the day before The Feast of The Assumption of Mary. He was beatified by Pope John Paul II in 1971 and canonized as a martyr on October 10,1982 also by Pope John Paul II.

St .Maximilian Kolbe was a great man dedicated to our blessed Catholic faith, Our Blessed Mother and Jesus. He worked to help people come to know Our Lord and Savior Jesus Christ. He died a
Martyr, standing up for the faith as Our Lady asked of him many years before.

Many of us will certainly never be martyrs for the Faith, but all of us can stand up to the faith and be witnesses as St. Maximilian. We can help and love our fellow man to be and to love as Jesus commands. May The Blessed Trinity be always in our mind, on our lips and in our hearts. Amen

Thank you all again for purchasing this book it has been a joy to write. I will be writing another volume of more Modern Saints soon.

If you have found favor with this book please leave me a review. I would greatly appreciate it. May God richly bless you always and May Jesus be Praised, Adored and Loved, now and forever.

I have written several other books you will be interested in too. They are listed below.

The Rosary for Children
http://www.amazon.com/The-Rosary-Children-Package-50/dp/1592763383/ref=sr_1_5?ie=UTF8&qid=1379776618&sr=8-5&keywords=andrea+maglio-macullar

The Mysteries of The Holy Rosary Illustrated
http://www.amazon.com/Mysteries-Holy-Rosary-Illustrated-ebook/dp/B00CFL8J78/ref=sr_1_4?ie=UTF8&qid=1379776618&sr=8-4&keywords=andrea+maglio-macullar

The Stations of the Cross for Everyone
http://www.amazon.com/The-Stations-Cross-Everyone-ebook/dp/B00CH7GKMQ/ref=sr_1_8?ie=UTF8&qid=1379776618&sr=8-8&keywords=andrea+maglio-macullar

Ray the T/A (Trans Am) (Illustrated this one) My Brother wrote it.
http://www.amazon.com/Ray-the-T-A-ebook/dp/B00CLW3BUG/ref=sr_1_2?ie=UTF8&qid=1379776618&sr=8-2&keywords=andrea+maglio-macullar

Garden Light, In Paint (Original Paintings) This book has a new bonus addition. Lots of Colorful Garden Paintings

Easy Painting with Gouache Watercolorshttp://www.amazon.com/Easy-Painting-Gouache-Watercolors-ebook/dp/B00E2T1CLQ/ref=sr_1_7?ie=UTF8&qid=1379776618&sr=8-7&keywords=andrea+maglio-macullar
This book will be interesting to folks who would like to learn to paint. Do You want to learn how to paint? Then this book is for you. Andrea is an award winning painter and in this book she will teach any artists that would like to learn to paint in an opaque paint medium. This includes acrylics and gouache. The author/artist uses gouache paint. She writes from her experience and will create 3 paintings, bringing the reader into her studio. She explains step by step how her paintings are created, with photos, showing you how. There will also be sections on the history of gouache paint. She explains what type of brushes would be best to use for painting. Also she goes on to talk about, the type of surface to paint on paper, canvas, etc. Also a simple way to creating a pleasing composition, and easy ways to mix color. She breaks down color mixing to show that it is not the difficult task, some beginner artist's think it is.

20 Best Italian Desserts by Noni Ida (Noni's Best Recipes (Illustrated and photographed) Great Italian Desserts for any occasion.

Andrea's newest illustrated book THE CAT THAT PURRED is in publication and will be released in the spring of 2014. A children's book published by New City Press. Watch for it!!

Please feel free to see more of my art work at my website

www.andsart.weebly.com   If you would like to contact me feel free to at my website also.

Printed in Great Britain
by Amazon